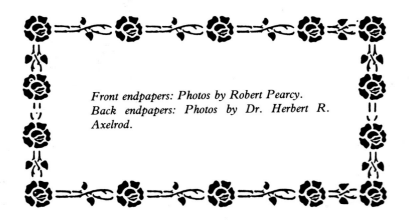

Front endpapers: Photos by Robert Pearcy.
Back endpapers: Photos by Dr. Herbert R.
Axelrod.

**To Candy, my sweetest
Poodle.**

A Beginner's Guide To
Poodles

Written By
Helen Telford

Contents

© 1986 by T.F.H. Publications, Inc. Distributed in the UNITED STATES by T.F.H. Publications, Inc., 211 West Sylvania Avenue, Neptune City, NJ 07753; in CANADA by H & L Pet Supplies Inc., 27 Kingston Crescent, Kitchener, Ontario N2B 2T6; Rolf C. Hagen Ltd., 3225 Sartelon Street, Montreal 382 Quebec; in CANADA to the Book Trade by Macmillan of Canada (A Division of Canada Publishing Corporation), 164 Commander Boulevard, Agincourt, Ontario M1S 3C7; in ENGLAND by T.F.H. Publications Limited, 4 Kier Park, Ascot, Berkshire SL5 7DS; in AUSTRALIA AND THE SOUTH PACIFIC by T.F.H. (Australia) Pty. Ltd., Box 149, Brookvale 2100 N.S.W., Australia; in NEW ZEALAND by Ross Haines & Son, Ltd., 18 Monmouth Street, Grey Lynn, Auckland 2 New Zealand; in SINGAPORE AND MALAYSIA by MPH Distributors (S) Pte., Ltd., 601 Sims Drive, #03/07/21, Singapore 1438; in the PHILIPPINES by Bio-Research, 5 Lippay Street, San Lorenzo Village, Makati Rizal; in SOUTH AFRICA by Multipet Pty. Ltd., 30 Turners Avenue, Durban 4001. Published by T.F.H. Publications, Inc. Manufactured in the United States of America by T.F.H. Publications, Inc.

1.
Introduction

The poodle is the attractive, lively Prince of Dogs. Whichever variety you choose, the Toy Poodle, the Miniature Poodle, or the Standard Poodle, you will have a pet who has won the hearts of dog lovers everywhere. Possessing incomparable style and a quick intelligence, he makes a loyal and aristocratic companion who will add joy to your household.

Except for size, all varieties of Poodles are judged by the same standard. Photo by Sally Ann Thompson.

Introduce your new Poodle to other pets in your household as soon as possible. They get used to each other and will stay friends. Photo by Sally Anne Thompson.

Scholars are still uncertain about the Poodle's origins, but it is a well-known fact that fifteenth-century European nobles considered him an excellent hunting dog. Through subsequent centuries his sterling qualities came to be appreciated all over the world. In recent years this intelligent breed has attained prominence in the demanding world of television and circus, and has been outstanding in obedience trials in the United States and England.

Since Poodles were used extensively for retrieving game from water, their heavy coats proved to be a hindrance. It became a common procedure to clip the legs and the rear half of the Poodle's coat leaving small tufts on the Poodle's joints and hocks. From a utilitarian practice, it soon became fashionable to clip Poodles in this style. Similarly, another fashion of tying up the "top knot" with a colorful ribbon rose from the need to locate the Poodle as he retrieved game in the water. Clipping the Poodle quickly became popular throughout Europe.

How a Poodle should look and act is described in what is called the "Standard" for the breed. Standards vary from time to time and place to place, so check with your national dog registry association to obtain up to date standards.

2.
Selection

Among dog enthusiasts it is readily acknowledged that owning a Poodle is a tribute to one's recognition of what is best. In the home his lively personality soon makes him a cherished member of the family. His aristocractic and elegant appearance graces your home with beauty. His unrestrained affection, sprightly intelligence, and persevering loyalty is a combination of qualities rarely to be found

The poodle is not a rare breed. It is possible to get one in almost any part of the world. This one was bred in Germany.

in any other citizen of the canine kingdom. Whether Toy, Miniature, or Standard, children easily fall in love with them; their natural clowning appeals to all.

Female and male Poodles differ slightly in temperament. Both are equally affectionate, but the male has a characteristic friskiness about him that many people like. Of course, if you like puppies or wish to breed Poodles, select a female. You will be able to feel like a proud grandparent and think of how happy your friends will be when you give them a cute Poodle puppy. Or, if you want to keep most the puppies, it will be like having another family. Buy a good female, select the best stud available and you may even realize a profit on your breeding.

His irresistible appeal

Some Poodle owners never had to choose their Poodle. A neighbor or close friend owned a Poodle who gave birth to a litter of lively pups. All that was necessary for these lucky people was to pick the one they liked best. But, if you are not so fortunate, you may find

Toy Poodles are just as sturdy as the other larger varieties of the breed.

10

In addition to the black and silver shown here, Poodles of other colors are recognized for showing. Photo by Sally Anne Thompson.

the right Poodle at a nearby kennel or pet shop. Your telephone book is the best place to find a list of kennels and pet shops specializing in Poodles. Similarly, dog magazines and your newspapers carry many useful advertisements.

Poodle puppies are so appealing that when you first see a litter the temptation to take one home may prove irresistible. Exercise careful judgment in selecting the puppy that is right for you. After looking at puppies in several pet shops or kennels, you will soon notice differences in temperament and appearance. Look for an active puppy, one that is bold, venturesome and full of mischief. In each litter there is one puppy who shows a zest for life and precociousness unequalled by his littermates.

Appearance is a good guide to a puppy's health. A puppy's eyes and ears should be clear. Check his teeth and gums. The upper teeth should project ever so slightly over the lower for a scissors bite. The gums should be a healthy pink. A firm, non-watery stool is a sign of his good health. Normally it is wise to choose a young puppy; he will adapt to a new environment more quickly.

11

The cost of Poodle puppies with pedigrees depends on the achievement and fame of the parents.

Most reputable pet shops and kennels allow you to take the puppy you have selected to a veterinarian for a general check up. Since the veterinarian will be one of your dog's best friends, his approval of your purchase is essential. If the veterinarian disapproves of your choice you will usually have the option of getting either a refund or another puppy.

3.
The new puppy

Your puppy should have a special place of his own. It can be anywhere, under a table, next to your bed, or beside a chair. His bed should be put away from drafts and dampness, preferably in a dark corner and large enough for him to curl up in. The bed can be a shallow cardboard box, a regular dog basket, or a bed purchased at your pet shop.

With proper grooming and clipping, these shaggy apricot Poodles will be transformed into real beauties. Photo by Sally Anne Thompson.

A pensive moment between active playing. Both young and old Poodles enjoy their toys.

14

Other things your puppy needs are two dishes, one for food and one for liquids. Make sure his toys are solid and hard.

Along with his bed, dishes, and toys, you will need a comb and brush. A strong steel comb with fine teeth at one end and medium teeth at the other will suffice. You will also need a stiff long wire-bristled brush (for Toy Poodles use the small size with rounded teeth.) Ask your pet supply dealer for information concerning types of collars, leashes and accessories which are especially suited to your Poodle.

With proper care and understanding your puppy's first night away from his mother, brothers and sisters should not be trying. In his new surroundings what he needs most is security. The "tick-tock" of a towel-wrapped clock in his bed will lessen any loneliness he may feel; a cloth doll will give him something warm to nestle to.

If you provide all possible comfort for him on his first night he will guickly grow to love his new home. Should he cry don't make the mistake of picking him up or petting him. He will then cry every time he wants to be petted. Show him from the beginning that crying will only result in stern disapproval.

Fuel for growth

Because your puppy's food is the fuel for his growth, you will want to plan a balanced diet for him. When you get a new pup, find out from his previous owner his feeding schedule and the type of food he has been getting. Like a child's, his stomach is sensitive to a sudden change in diet, so introduce any new food gradually, by adding small amounts of it to the food he's accustomed to. Gradually increase the amount of the new item while reducing the old until the changeover is complete.

Meat, boiled milk, or cottage cheese are essential to the diet of a young puppy. A nourishing grade of meal or kibble is an important part of the older pup's diet. Remember that the Standard and Miniature are much larger dogs than the Toy, and they can be fed food that should not be given to the Toy until he's five or six months old.

15

A young puppy being introduced to feeding from a dish as the mother watches nearby. Photo by Barbara Lockwood.

Your puppy is full of life and needs plenty of food to keep him active. Feed him four times daily, in the morning, noon, early evening, and night. After several months, he will begin to eye scraps of food on your table. Why don't you give him a tidbit? But NOT from the table. After you've finished your meal put it in his own dish, in its usual spot. Otherwise you'll have a beggar at the table and this can become a nuisance. He will also begin to like canned dog food and dry food moistened with milk, water or broth.

When your puppy is three months old you may begin to reduce the number of his daily meals. At this age, he is satisfied with three meals. But if he still wants another meal, don't refuse it. At six months reduce the feedings to twice daily. Within a few months, at one year old, he will be eating one meal a day and then you will know that your puppy has grown up! Toy Poodles, because of their small size, sometimes find it difficult to maintain adequate body reserves. Extra meals, particularly during the critical first six months, are very beneficial.

16

Chef's choice

Picking the right dog food is a problem for all dog owners. You have seen many brands of dog biscuits selling at different prices. Some of the biscuits are made from manufacturer's by-products. Others are top grade wheat bought solely to be used as flour in dog biscuits.

Check the amount of protein a brand of dog food contains before you buy it. The package that has the highest percentage of protein for the money is always the best buy. It is always best to buy your Poodle food with a high protein content.

Carbohydrates, fats, vitamins and minerals also play an important role in your Poodle's diet. Dog biscuits are a good source of carbohydrates. Fats are obtained from lard, lamb, fish, chicken, suet, vegetable oils, and bacon fat. Reputable manufacturers of dog food make sure their products contain all the vitamins your Poodle needs. If your Poodle has a balanced diet his mineral needs will also be well taken care of.

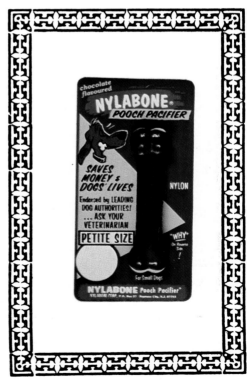

The Petite size of Nylabone® is ideal for puppies and adult Miniature and Toy Poodles. A Standard Poodle can manage a slightly bigger one.

There will be times when your Poodle will not want to eat at all. Like a human, he may simply not be hungry. Take his food away after about fifteen minutes. This may revive his appetite for the next meal.

Housebreaking

Housebreaking is helping your puppy to become a member of the family. Poodles naturally like to be clean and the sooner you provide a special place for yours the happier he will be. When placing newspapers in his enclosed area—and don't skimp—be affectionate, and tell him this spot belongs to him. Give him loving pats as a sign of your approval when he relieves himself upon the newspaper. If he starts to make a mistake, rush him to the newspaper to complete the job there.

After a few days begin to reduce the number of newspaper pages until you are down to one or two. The pup will soon get the idea that the single newspaper is his one and only spot. The odor of a slightly soiled newspaper will attract him. Commercial products are available with which to scent fresh newspaper as an indication of where he is to go.

Your adorable Toy Poodle deserves a jeweled collar for special occasions. Choose one that is well made and cannot snag your pet's thick fur.

Portrait of a healthy Poodle. Note the alert appearance, bright and clear eyes, and apparent intelligence of this dog. Photo by Dr. Herbert R. Axelrod.

Nature calls to a puppy after meals. If the weather is bad, let him use his place indoors, but if weather permits always take him outside. This applies, of course, to the very young pup. The older one should be taken out regardless of the weather. As soon as he has relieved himself outside, bring him back in immediately. Returning him home quickly will teach him the purpose of these trips.

Housebreaking your pup, if carried out with moderation, affection, and patience, achieves long-lasting results. Whenever you are training him remember that, like people, puppies need understanding— an attitude highly essential for later training.

Getting along with people

The essence of the word PET is ". . . getting along with people . . ."If he is to be your friend and companion, your pet must learn his name. This can be accomplished during the house-breaking period. Select a short name for him and use it every time you address him. It should be distinctive and not sound like any other name in the household. He will quickly learn to recognize it. When he responds to it, reward him with a caress or a tidbit.In the

The handling of a Poodle by a child should be properly supervised. Photo by Tom Caravaglia.

A lovely garden provides a beautiful setting for a pair of well behaved Poodles. Photo by Barbara Lockwood.

early stage of all his training, call him by name frequently, and always reward him when he responds.

No question about it, your frisky and inquisitive pup will sometimes hop up on the furniture. From the beginning, you must make clear to him that your sofa, couch, table, etc., are offbounds. A sharp rebuke will soon teach him to keep away. When he is teething, you should not leave wallets, shoes, rubbers, and slippers carelessly around the house. Purchase a Nylon bone such as Nylabone®, available at your local pet shop. In a short time, he will have lost his enthusiasm for chewing anything else.

Patient, attentive and loving

The key to Poodle training lies in your attitude. Both of you will have a pleasant time if you remain patient, attentive, loving and persistent in your efforts. Make him feel that his training has meaning. Such rewards as small tidbits of food, companionship, a satisfying grooming, will interest him in learning new things. The basis of all training may be summed up in these words: Don't give a command unless you can enforce it! Once you have given an order make sure that it is obeyed!

The exuberance of a Poodle during play is demonstrated in this photo very well. However, such displays must be controlled by good training at an early age. Photo by Sally Anne Thompson.

It requires a little time for a dog to get a clear idea of what you want him to accomplish. You must be prepared to repeat your commands until you are sure he understands. Praise him and reward him when he does well. Poodles are intelligent and anxious to learn.

4.
Obedience

Your Poodle should be taught the simple rules of obedience. They consist of the commands: "Come," "Sit," "Down," and "Heel." Outdoors your dog will naturally want to go off and play with other dogs or chase birds and cats. For his own safety and your peace of mind, he should be taught to walk close to you. How do you teach him this? Purchase a comfortable leash and collar for him. Let him sniff the collar. Then praise him lavishly as you put it on.

Poodles are born entertainers. They are still used as circus performers today.

A trio of perfectly trained Miniature Poodles posed for this photo. Such coopera-tion is not possible with untrained Poodles. Photo by Sally Anne Thompson.

After he is used to it, take him out for a stroll. He may prefer to linger behind and will pull or plunge against the lead. After a few steps, stop and pull him to your left side while calling him by name. When he reaches you, praise and pet him until he quiets down. Then start off again, calling him as you go, until he learns to follow in the direction the leash tugs. He will soon discover that it is useless to struggle and more comfortable to walk along than be dragged. Each time he ceases to struggle, pet him and reward him. When he becomes frightened, reassure him. Soon he will learn to look forward to these strolls and to associate the leash with them.

To come

Learning to come when called by voice or whistle is next. Do not expect your pup to pick up this accomplishment immediately. Take him outside. Attach a light check cord at least twenty feet long to his collar. Allow him to have a short romp. When his attention has become attracted to something else, call him by name and give him the command "Come". When he responds, pat him, reward him, and allow him to continue his romp, calling him to you at intervals.

Soon he will become tired of having his pleasure interfered with and will refuse to come when ordered. Grasp the end of the check cord, repeat the command "Come", and give the cord a sharp jerk. He will probably try to resist, but keep repeating the command. A few sharp jerks will bring him to you. Reward him with a tidbit and caress. Repeat this several times before you end the lesson.

Never allow a lesson to go on too long. This training may be repeated several times a day, but having him come to you three or four times in each session is enough. Never, under any circumstances call your dog to you for punishment. If punishment or scolding is necessary, go to him. When you call, he should always know that something pleasant is going to happen—if only a pat on the head.

To sit

With the dog standing in front of you or by your side, hold the leash in your right hand and give the command 'Sit". At the same time lean over and with your left hand press down steadily on his rump until he is in a sitting position. Slip a tidbit in his mouth and

Show dogs are trained to stand still for judging. Unruly dogs are penalized in the show ring. Photo by Tom Caravaglia.

praise him. Repeat this ritual several times, using the same command and pressing down on his rump. Soon he will associate the command with the pressure and anticipate it by sitting without being touched. You can then begin keeping him in a sitting position for longer periods of time.

"Down": After you have taught him to "Sit", it is not very difficult to teach him what "Down" means. Holding your pet by the collar with one hand, give the command "Down". Press on his rump with the other. When he is sitting, use the right hand to pull his front feet out from under him while you press down on his shoulder with the left hand and repeat the command "Down". Give the command "Up" when you allow him to rise. As you give the command take a few steps and he'll "Up" to follow you. Repetition of this practice will soon teach the dog to go down at the command "Down". You may raise you hand while you are voicing the command. Finally, all that is needed to cause the dog to drop down is to bring the hand into a raised position. The dog can be taught to remain "Down" for long periods if desired.

Retrieving is a natural activity for a Poodle. A ball is ideal for this exercise. Photo by Sally Anne Thompson.

A young Poodle impeccably groomed for a formal portrait. Photo by Robert Pearcy.

27

A whimsical photo of three Poodles getting dry after a bath. This procedure is definitely not recommended. Photo by Barbara Lockwood.

To "Heel"

This is the correct way to walk a mature dog. The loop of the leash is held in your right hand, the thong passes across your body to the dog who is on your left; control the slack of the leash with your left hand, shortening it or lengthening it as necessary.

Say clearly, "Rover, heel!" and start out with your left foot. When the dog strains ahead, jerk back sharply with your left hand but let the leash slacken instantly. Never pull the dog back into position; never drag him forward. It accomplishes nothing. The quick jerk is what does it. It makes him momentarily uncomfortable and he quickly learns that if he walks correctly at your left knee there will be no jerk. Keep walking, keep repeating "Heel", keep jerking when necessary. Remember to praise him when he walks properly. You'll be surprised how quickly he learns.

5.
Grooming

The bath: While dog experts argue pro and con whether dogs should be bathed regularly or not, the fact of the matter is that there are going to be times when your Poodle will need a bath. Make it no oftener than once a month unless there's an emergency—like his climbing out of a coal bin, for instance. Never give him a bath before he's six months old. You can use one of the com-

For appearance and comfort a Poodle is clipped. However,
show Poodles are generally clipped and groomed
professionally in preparation for a competition.

mercially prepared aerosol foam baths to give a pup a dry cleaning. The foam is simply sprayed on and toweled off. These dry baths are particularly useful in winter.

The bath water should be roughly the same as the dog's own temperature, about 101°F. It should be deep enough to touch his underbody when he stands upright in the tub. A rubber-hose portable spray will come in handy for wetting him down and rinsing him. Use a soap or shampoo designed for dogs, working the lather well down into the skin because that is where the real dirt is. Do not use any soap on his head. Merely wipe it and his muzzle and ears off with a damp washcloth, making very sure that no suds get into the eyes, ears, or nose. Overdo the rinsing to make sure you get out every bit of soap. Then after allowing him one vigorous shake wrap him up in an old towel and rub him vigorously to stimulate the circulation. A portable hair dryer can be used for the finishing touches, or he can be exercised indoors if it's cold out, outdoors if the weather is warm.

To keep the ear fringes and top knot of this apricot show Poodle in perfect condition, the hair is rolled in fabric. Photo by Sally Anne Thompson.

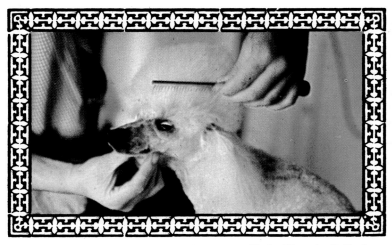

Combing up the topknot for an impressive crown of hair. Photo by Sally Anne Thompson.

A deft touch

A Poodle owner accepts the responsiblity of either grooming his pet at home or sending him to a beauty parlor. Grooming a Poodle requires practice and artistry. All experts agree that only professional Poodle trimmers can do a superlative job of trimming. One reason for such a claim is that show judges accept only three types of clipping—all requiring an extremely deft touch. Most owners, however, prefer Poodle clips that are more simple.

If you have decided to groom your Poodle at home, you will need the following special grooming tools:

    Clippers: with fine, medium, coarse and skip-tooth
      blades
    Scissors: blunt and sharp
    Rake
    Nail Clippers
    Tweezers
    Wire Brush

A newly groomed Poodle in the Royal Dutch clip. This style is easy to keep neat in appearance and is quite popular.

THE WORLD'S LARGEST SELECTION OF PET, ANIMAL, AND MUSIC BOOKS.

T.F.H. Publications publishes more than 900 books covering many hobby aspects (dogs, cats, birds, fish, small animals, music, etc.). Whether you are a beginner or an advanced hobbyist you will find exactly what you're looking for among our complete listing of books. For a free catalog fill out the form on the other side of this page and mail it today.

. . . BIRDS . .

. . CATS . . .

. . . ANIMALS . . .

. . . DOGS . . .

. . FISH . . .

. . . MUSIC . . .

For more than 30 years, *Tropical Fish Hobbyist* has been the source of accurate, up-to-the-minute, and fascinating information on every facet of the aquarium hobby.

Join the more than 50,000 devoted readers worldwide who wouldn't miss a single issue.

Only the trial and error of experience can teach you how to use clippers. As for the blunt scissors, they are used to clip the hair around the Poodle's ears and face. The other pair of scissors has a sharp point used for cutting tiny hairs between the toes and for overall trimming. The rake is used to remove mats and tangles from his coat. The nail clippers must be used very carefully to avoid cutting a blood vessel. Use a stiff brush with long wire bristles. The tweezers are necessary to remove the hair from his ears.

Styles of simple clipping

A simple clip for beginners is the Lamb clip. The Poodle is clipped close on the body and neck. The legs are trimmed moderately full. Both the tail pompon and the top knot are well defined. The Lamb clip is very attractive and can be easily altered to correct any mistakes a beginner might make.

The most popular clip in America is the Dutch. The stately top knot, tail pompon and partially full body make this a particularly distinguished style. The legs are full. The feet are clipped clean around the dewclaw mark. One stripe follows the spine and another which should reach forward on the underside, runs about his midsection. There are a considerable number of variations of this clip of which the Royal Dutch is the easiest to maintain.

The Riviera Clip is highly elegant and somewhat similar to the Continental Clip. Its main characteristics are leg bracelets and a closely shaved rear. There are other attractive clips which bear such exotic names as the Palm Springs, the Las Vegas and the Kerry. These are often used by Poodle fanciers who have no intention of entering their dogs for show.

Clip the nails gingerly

Watching your Poodle romping in the open on wide grassy spaces, giving vent to all his energy, exercising his freedom to his heart's content is a joyful sight to behold. However, no matter how much you let him romp, if he does not get the chance to exercise on concrete or gravel, his nails will need attention.

A Poodle that is familiar with the clipping process will seldom fuss or fidget on the grooming table. Photo by Sally Anne Thompson.

Try to make his clipping as quick and pleasant as possible. Keep him absolutely still to eliminate the danger of nipping a blood vessel. Every time you bring your pet to the veterinarian, he may, if you wish, clip the nails. While you're there, ask him for some tips on clipping. To reduce the number of clippings, you should file the points of his nails every two or three weeks with a flat wood-file. The file should be drawn in only one direction from the top of the nail downward in a round stroke to the end of the nail or underneath. Considerable pressure is needed for a few strokes in order to get through the hard polished surface of the nail.

Grooming for the bench

Once your Poodle has been entered for the show, the next step is to groom him according to the established rules. The uninitiated may look with some misgiving upon the first Poodle they see with full-bloom coat clipped in the height of fashion. This is a long-time Poodle practice which is neither a fad nor impractical. It has certainly enhanced the dog's looks, and in no way has affected his character or abilities.

The following description is of the English Saddle Clip. In the Continental Clip the scissored saddle is clipped bare except for rosettes on the hips.

The Feet

Clip the foot in its entirety, on top, underneath and between the toes. Start the lower bracelet about an inch above the toes.

The First Bracelet

At a point just above the hock, clip a band completely around the leg of an inch or two in width. In deciding on the width, be guided by the size of the dog and your own personal preference. This band or line must be parallel to the lower band above the toes and at a right angle with the leg. This completes the first bracelet and forms the lower line for the second bracelet.

The Second Bracelet

This should extend to the first thigh joint. The upper and lower lines must be parallel. Be sure to clip the inside of the leg.

Comb out small snarls before they become unmanageable and will require professional attention.

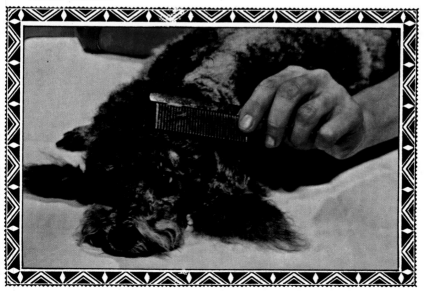

The Rear Coat

With the bracelets finished, the lower line of the saddle or "pants" has been formed. This should extend about an inch or an inch and a half below the crotch. Before the saddle is blocked out, the remaining rear coat should be cut with scissors to about one inch in length, trimming forward to the second or third from rear. If the dog has a long back, leave more ruff.

The Saddle

Begin the saddle point at the center of the spine, about an inch back of the ruff. In clipping, go back and downward. Miss the hip bone by about an inch. Move forward and downward toward the brisket to a point just back of the ruff, tapering as you go. Square this sharply, clipping a band parallel with the point at the center of the back, making it about an inch in width. Clip the other side the same way, making sure your design is correct.

It will be necessary to square off the lower edge of the "pants" with the scissors. Use the scissors on the saddle to get the hair to about three-fourths of an inch in length. The under part of the dog, back of the ruff, is clipped bare.

The Tail

The tail should be clipped from its base so that a pompon about three inches in length remains at the tip. Round off the pompon.

The Front Puffs

These should consist of a strip of coat about three inches wide. They should start about an inch above the toes. The legs should be clipped close above the puff.

The Head

Clip away from the eyes, not towards them. Clip out the end of the muzzle from the inner corner of the eye. Clean the cheeks well, clipping all intervening space. Clip an arc downward from the base

The care given by a concerned Poodle owner is reflected in the appearance of his or her pet. Photo by Fritz Prenzel.

This Poodle is learning how to pose for a show. Photo by Sally Anne Thompson.

of the ear to the center of the neck, about four or five inches below the lower jaw. Be sure to get both sides even. Clip under the jaw and the part of the throat desired.

The Finish

The finishing touches add much to the neatness of the job. The bracelets and puffs should be scissored to about two inches in length. With comb and scissors square them where they appear to need it, so that they follow the natural lines of the leg structure.

It will also be necessary to square off the lower edge of the "pants" with the scissors. Use the scissors on the saddle to get the hair to about three-fourths of an inch in length. The under part of the dog, back of the ruff, is clipped bare. It is in the finishing touches that the artistry of the trimmer is evidenced.

The Puppy Clip

The only acceptable show clip for puppies requires little grooming. A puppy's hair is too delicate for any pattern. A clipped face, feet, tail, stomach, and hair slightly trimmed to give a neat appearance, typify the Puppy Clip.

6.
Care

Dogs are very much like people in many respects. While proper food, shelter, exercise and sanitation are all very essential to the health and good temperament of a dog, attention, companionship and affection also play an important part in his well-being. Poodles are hardy individuals, able to adapt themselves to almost any living conditions. Pampering is unnecessary and should for the dog's own

An international champion like Pixiecroft Krusader shown here is the result of good pedigree, rigorous training and meticulous care. Photo by Tom Caravaglia.

sake be avoided. This does not mean, however, that he is not entitled to the attention of his master.

Every dog owner should spend at least a little time every day with his pet, in addition to looking after his necessities. Of course, if the dog is kept in the house, he sees much of the family and becomes part of it. But if he is kept in a kennel, he should be removed from his confines at least once daily, given a period of exercise on a leash and if possible, a good romp in an open space where he is not likely to get into mischief. These periods can be employed to train your Poodle in the niceties of behavior. They allow time for a good brisk grooming so essential to the development and maintenance of a good healthy coat and skin.

First aid

Most of the time your Poodle is able to take care of himself. Generally, he will lick a small cut or wound and it will heal. However, you may treat such small wounds as you would your own. Thoroughly clean the wound and apply a mild antiseptic or first aid cream.

A simple bed equates to security for any breed of dog. Be sure your Poodle's bed is situated away from drafts. Photo by Sally Anne Thompson.

Playful encounters with the family cat can result in scratches. If any, these should be treated immediately before possible infection sets in.

However, he cannot remove a thorn from his paw, or a burr from his coat, nor can he set a broken leg. Remember, if your dog is hurt, he will be looking to you for help. Don't become overly excited. Carefully examine him before you move him. If he has a broken bone you must apply a splint before moving him. Keeping the leg as straight as possible, attach a splint to the leg by tying it above and below the break.

Nearly all dogs hurt in accidents suffer from shock. The heart beats faster but weaker and they often seem oblivious to pain. Shock needs treatment before any minor cuts or breaks are given attention. It is best treated by covering the dog with a warm blanket and keeping him warm. If he can swallow, the simplest household stimulant to administer is coffee with sugar and cream and a pinch of salt. Gently lift his head, loosen the muzzle and pour the coffee into a pocket made by pulling out his lip.

After any treatment, notify the veterinarian. If he thinks you can handle it he will tell you so.

The spread of most communicable diseases among dogs is controlled by the proper immunization at the right time. Photo by Anne Sally Thompson.

Cuts

The feet of dogs have numerous small blood vessels which can bleed profusely from even a small cut. Should the cut be severe or the blood flow difficult to staunch, you may wish to apply a tourniquet between the cut and the heart. Relax the pressure for a few seconds every five or ten minutes. A normal cut needs only a pressure bandage. This should be firmly applied to help create a blood clot. Should the bandage be applied too loosely, it will merely sponge up blood rather than prevent the flow. Leave this bandage on until a clot seems to have formed.

It may be necessary for the veterinarian to suture the cut. This will help the wound heal and can have your Poodle as active as ever in ten days or less. Just make sure a clean bandage is applied every second day.

Accidental poisoning and antidotes

Poisoned animals require immediate attention. Administer first aid measures before rushing him to the vet's. If you know the poison, apply the antidote listed on the label of the container. However if you are not sure, use the following general procedure.

Empty his stomach by giving him a 3% solution of hydrogen peroxide mixed half-and-half with water. A tablespoon for each ten pounds of dog is required. This turns into oxygen and water inside his stomach, causing him to vomit, but is otherwise harmless. It takes about two minutes to act. Let his stomach settle and then give him some Epsom salts, a teaspoonful in some water to empty his bowels quickly.

The hydrogen peroxide is an antidote for phosphorus, while Epsom salts are proper medication against lead poisoning. A third antidote that can be given that is effective against two other poisons is the "hypo" used in photographic darkrooms. A teaspoonful in water is sufficient.

However, try to determine the poison and apply proper rather than expedient antidotes.

Poodles like to jump during play. They instinctively know how to land properly and seldom have fractures or dislocations.

Clear colors are preferred in show Poodles, but tipping or shading is allowed in some colors. Photo by Fritz Prenzel.

7.
Ailments

As do people, dogs have their ups and downs. But a dog who has had a proper series of inoculations, a steady and nourishing diet, plenty of exercise, has had clean quarters and a daily brushing is likely to remain a healthy dog. When concerned about your dog's health, a good axiom to keep in mind is, "An ounce of prevention is worth a pound of cure." Knowing the symptoms of common dis-

Silver Poodles are born black, but the coat gradually lightens with age. Photo by Sally Anne Thompson.

eases will enable you to spot them immediately and to give the veterinarian a general idea of what is wrong. Following is a list of common ailments.

Diarrhea

This is a common ailment. A change of diet, excitement and improper feeding are the usual causes. Give your dog Kaopectate or milk of bismuth. A teaspoonful to a tablespoon every three hours, the quantity depends on the size of your dog. If his condition persists, consult your veterinarian.

Constipation

A diet of rich and starchy foods may harden in the bowels. Your dog needs plenty of roughage, exercise and ample opportunity for relieving himself. These simple measures can usually solve the worst constipation problem. But if it persists, use milk of magnesia or mineral oil. If there are no results call your veterinarian.

Avoid cutting the quick of your Poodle's toenails. For safety, do not trim them too deep. Photo by Sally Anne Thompson.

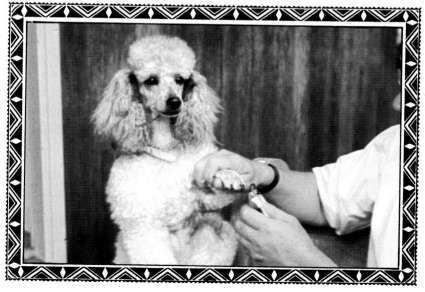

Keep a watchful eye on the appearance and temperament of your Poodle. Signs of illness are not too difficult to recognize. Photo by Tom Caravaglia.

Distemper

True distemper, which is correctly called Carre's disease after the man who studied it, is seldom seen today thanks to our advanced methods of immunization. However, the word distemper is frequently used in a generic sense to indicate a dog with a generalized set of symptoms. Used in this way the prognosis might vary from good to fair to poor, depending on what is actually causing the symptoms.

There are a number of problems occurring in puppies the symptoms of which, particularly in their early stages, are very similar, and accurate diagnosis is almost impossible. These symptoms include elevated temperature, mucousy nose and/or eyes, loss of appetite, diarrhea, listlessness, frequent productive sneezing, vomiting and a deep cough, low in the abdomen, as distinguished from a bronchial cough which is in the upper region.

These symptoms alone alone are sufficient to suspect distemper although, by themselves, they do not support a positive diagnosis as many other, less serious diseases will frequently cause the same symptoms.

47

A brisk rubdown with a big towel ensures freedom from chills. Photo by Sally Anne Thompson.

Additional symptoms more characteristic of true distemper are photophobia, or fear of light, a distinctive temperature curve and conjunctivitis. The puppy will hide in dimly lit areas and, when exposed to light, will squint and show his discomfort. Another distinctive symptom is the so-called diphasic, or saddle, curve of temperature. From the normal of 101 to 102.2°F. the puppy's temperature will shoot up as high as 105°F. on the fifth day after infection, followed by a rise to 103 to 104°F. and it remains approximately that for the duration of the disease.

Conjunctivitis is an inflammation of the conjunctiva, the membranes lining the eyelids.

Frequently, sores are seen on the stomach. The skin, when pinched, retains the crease, returning slowly to normal in contrast to the skin of a healthy dog which snaps back.

In the early stages keep the puppy warm and check its temperature daily keeping a written record. This will help your veterinarian make a positive diagnosis should the symptoms persist. Give medicine only as prescribed by the veterinarian and the puppy should be hand-fed if necessary. Boil 4 oz of milk and 4 oz of water and allow them to cool. Add 2 oz of Karo syrup, the yolk of an egg and a pinch of salt and mix well. Give to the puppy freely. Should you have to resort to spoon-feeding, pull out the lips at the side to form a pocket and pour in a spoonful at a time. Allow ample time for it to go down before giving another. Make sure he gets nourishment often.

Simple diarrhea can be controlled by administering Kaopectate or milk of bismuth. For small puppies, give one tablespoon initially, followed by one teaspoon every three hours, or after every movement. For larger dogs increase the dosage in proportion to his size.

Should symptoms persist you must, of course, contact your veterinarian. However, do not become unduly discouraged. While distemper, when it does appear, is extremely serious, antibiotics help control the secondary infection and with good nursing there is a decent percentage of cures. Some, but by no means all, puppies are left with aftereffects which might range from hardly noticeable to severe, but many do make a complete recovery. Should it turn out

The teeth and mouth should be examined regularly. Dental problems are best treated by a veterinarian. Photo by Sally Anne Thompson.

that it wasn't true distemper after all, but one of the other puppy ailments, chances are good for a complete recovery.

Vaccination

Today the science of immunization has developed to a remarkable degree. Puppies can be given a long-lasting immunity to distemper by the time that they are ten weeks old. Your veterinarian can also inoculate your puppy with antibodies which, while their effect is measured in days, will serve to protect him until he can receive his permanent inoculation. At the same time that he is giving the distemper shots, your veterinarian may also immunize your puppy against hepatitis and leptospirosis. We will not go into a description of these diseases here as, in the early stages, their symptoms are similar to those described for distemper. An accurate diagnosis had best be left to your veterinarian who is trained to differentiate.

Be safe—have your puppy immunized before any symptoms appear as the value of inoculation, once he has contracted the disease, is doubtful.

Size range in Poodes: left to right, Standard, Miniature and Toy. Photo by Ake Wintzell.

Tracheobronchitis

"Kennel Cough" or tracheobronchitis is a mild ailment affecting puppies. They appear to be attempting to clear their throat and produce a gagging cough that is usually most severe during the night. Otherwise, the pup appears normal and both his appetite and bowel movements are as the should be. Eyes and nose are clear and his temperature ranges between 101 to 102.2°F. which is normal. "Kennel Cough", though not serious, is a highly contagious illness that is prevalent where puppies are kept in crowded quarters.

Luckily, "Kennel Cough" is a self-limiting disease. Pups usually recover without medication although they may have their rasping cough for as long as forty days. Nevertheless, cough mixtures may help alleviate the symptoms and these can be purchased at pet counters. Should the cough be severe or last an abnormal length of time, your veterinarian can prescribe sulfa drugs or one of the antibiotics (such as chloromycetin).

Tooth disorders

Your Poodle should be allowed to gnaw large bones, hard rubber toys and nylon bones such as Nylabone to keep his teeth strong and clean. Where discoloration shows, wipe the teeth with hydrogen peroxide and a piece of cloth. Toothpaste mixed with powdered pumice can also be used.

Eye care

The eyes should be watched carefully. After each romp into high grass or cover, weed seeds and foreign matter should be flushed out with warm water, because the presence of such material is exceedingly irritating and may cause serious damage. A commercially prepared eyewash can be found at most pet shops for general care of the eyes.

Common cold

The symptoms of the cold are similar in dog and human, although your pet is likely to suffer from loose bowels. Kaopectate will take care of this. Terramycin works wonders with dogs colds: as this drug is available only on prescription you must ask your veterinarian for it.

In the last fifteen years veterinary science has improved to such a degree that most of the major dog diseases can be cared for successfully.

Ear canker

The Poodle that paws and scratches his ears occasionally might have an ear infection, or might be scratching for the joy of scratching. Persistent scratching calls for a careful inspection. Check the ears for a brown, waxy substance that is a sign of ear canker. If not corrected promptly, it might become troublesome. Take a cotton swab, dip in it olive oil and remove as much of this secretion as possible. A commercially prepared medicated ear wash, available in most pet shops, is quite effective when used as directed.

Clean the ears frequently, but carefully. Serious troubles will require the services of a veterinarian. Photo by Sally Anne Thompson.

A Poodle bitch will require nourishing food before and after whelping. She can have her regular diet after the puppies are weaned.

Worms and worming

Even the best-cared-for dogs sometimes get worms. But not all worms are the same. There are roundworms, hookworms, whipworms, and tapeworms, just to name a few. Each requires its own special treatment. So be sure to consult your veterinarian for diagnosis and treatment. Symptoms: Actual appearance of the worm or segments of it in stools and vomit, A "potbelly", diarrhea, persistent vomiting, runny eyes and nose.

Roundworms: These worms, common in puppies, are fortunately fairly easy to get rid of. They are quite long, white or pinkish, tend to coil up like watchsprings—hence their name. Easily used and effective medication for roundworms will be found at the pet shop.

If you are not sure of the kind of worm which is infecting your dog, take a sample of his stool to the vet's for microscopic examination, and then let him prescribe the treatment.

Fleas

This problem must be attacked on two fronts. You have not only to rid your dog of the fleas and eggs infesting his body, you must also exterminate the eggs which have dropped off in those areas where he moves and sleeps. Use a good commercial flea powder or aerosol spray, following the directions on the container. Then completely disinfect his quarters and bed. This done, go over the dog with a brush and fine comb, getting rid of all the dead or dying parasites. Never neglect a dog's fleas or ticks. They are the cause of serious skin problems.

8.
Breeding

To the real dog-lover, there is no happier sight than that of a healthy and contented mother with an attractive litter of Poodle puppies. Your joy is even greater when you know these are the offspring of your own beloved pet. Your participation in the daily life and growth of a happy litter of Poodle puppies will be sure to fascinate you.

A Toy Poodle puppy and a Standard Poodle. Intersize crossing in Poodles is possible, but it can result in whelping problems in later generations and is not desirable. Photo by Sally Anne Thompson.

Healthy Poodle puppies are alert, active and frisky. Keep valuable items out of their way, and better yet, confine them in a pen or large cage. Photo by Barbara Lockwood.

If you already have a female, let nature assert herself at least once or twice during your female's lifetime. Giving birth and rearing a litter is the natural fulfillment of her life. After having successfully completed her motherly chores, she will become more mature in many ways; healthier, more obedient and loyal. Just make sure that you have good homes waiting for your puppies. If you don't, don't breed your Poodle.

Once you have decided to breed a litter you may be fortunate enough to obtain the services of a friend's Poodle or one of your neighbor's pets. If not, you will have to make arrangements with a professional breeder. The cost of his stud fee ranges from $50 to $250. Before mating, you must make sure your female has booster shots, worming checks and an excellent diet with a full complement of vitamins. If your dog is of exceptionally fine quality you should carefully check a stud's background to see how consistently he has won.

Your female will carry her young for about nine weeks. There are many warning signs to indicate that the moment is near. She will often seem restless and may decide to sleep in a new and strange place. She will aimlessly scratch at her bedding and become pre-occupied with licking or biting herself. A drop in temperature is a sure indication that birth is near. Give your veterinarian due warning and then let nature take its course, trying not to upset your mother-to-be.

A Standard's normal litter is approximately six to eight puppies.

A Miniature Poodle's normal litter is about three to five, although they may have as few as one or as many as eleven. For the first few days after giving birth, your female should be kept on a light diet of easily digestible foods, such as milk, cheese and broth. On the second or third day you may include some boiled fish, followed with a diet of boiled meats and possibly cooked eggs, until the end of the week when she is back on her normal schedule.

Between the third and sixth day your puppies should have their tails docked and their dewclaws removed. At this age they are too young to feel anything but minimal discomfort and healing is rapid. You will save yourself and the mother unnecessary anxiety by keeping her away from the scene of this minor operation.

Remember that your Poodles are happiest when they are with you. It may be difficult to have all your Poodles in the house with you at the same time. Why not alternate them—keeping one in your house while the others remain in the kennel. This will keep your dogs happy and it will show them that you love all of them equally.

Choose your puppies' new home with care!!

Thanks to the pioneering studies of heredity by the nineteeth–century monk, Gregory Mendel, the breeding of dogs has become a science. Without his "Law of Alternate Inheritance" the incredible advance in our knowledge of heredity in the last fifty years would have been impossible. Mendel's work desribed the inheritance of certain traits in plants as possessing a dominant and recessive relationship. The application of Mendel's Law to dogs is easily demonstrated by the following example:

A breeder mates a pure black Poodle to a white Poodle. As white is a recessive color we know that it cannot conceal black which is dominant. A friend has made the same kind of mating. All the puppies will be black, but they will be carrying genes for white. They each raise the pups to adulthood. Then they decide to mate a pup from one litter with a pup from the other. The pups from this mating should be 75% black and 25% white. Of the blacks, one third of them will be pure black while the others will be carrying genes for white.

The puppies from this cross of two hybrids may actually be all of one color or the other or even a different proportion than we expected. But our case doesn't contradict Mendel's Law. It simply shows there weren't enough pups for the mathematical expectancy to be realized. It is just as if we took a black and a white marble which one parent contributed and dropped them in a hat; then took two more which the other parent contributed. You'd have two black and two white marbles. Reach into the hat now and take out two. Record the color. Put them back, mix them and take out two more. Keep doing it and record what you had each time until you have drawn out 100 pairs. You will find you have very close to 25 times drawn a pair of white, 25 times drawn a pair of black and 50 times a pair composed of one black and one white. Now you might draw a pair of black several times in a row, but the great average is 25-50-25.

Thus, in any one litter the exact expectancy is not always realized, but there is an expectancy, nonetheless. It is governed by the "Law of Alternate Inheritance". This question of skipping a generation is now, as we have seen, mathematically explainable.

9.
Playing

As your Poodle becomes older and more mature, you and he can become true companions. The Poodle is capable of a loyalty unique among dogs. His intelligence is humanlike in many ways. Poodle fanciers say that their pets always seem to know in advance what the human wants to do next. The next time you see a person walking with his Poodle, notice how the two are attuned to each other.

Free from a leash, this Poodle in "action" is really having great fun.

A friendship so deep, so profound develops between master and pet, that only the word "affinity" can do justice to it.

Poodles are the embodiment of perkiness; they are the essence of "dogs". Ever see a Poodle at a picnic? They romp around for hours and when thrown a ball they retrieve with a truly professional style. Never miss watching a Poodle the first time he bounces into water. The grace with which he shakes off the water after he finishes his swim confirms his position as Prince of the Canine Kingdom.

His natural playfulness will make it easy for you to teach your pet a few mutually entertaining tricks. To teach him to shake hands, have him sit and give the command "Shake" clearly while lifting his right paw and shaking it. Immediately reward him with a piece of dog candy. Repeat this several times a day. Within a week he will greet you in the morning with a raised paw.

Teaching him to beg is done in a similar manner. Command him to sit and lift his paws to the begging position. Repetition will enable him to learn his trick within a few weeks.

Poodles love to retrieve. Buy a hard rubber ball or Nylaball at a reputable pet shop. Your dog can carry such toys safely in his mouth. If he doesn't immediately respond when you throw the ball, take him to the spot where the toy landed and return with it to your original position. Once he catches on, you can increase the distance you throw. Retrieving is a good way of exercising him and in getting to be pals with him.

Children and Poodles get along remarkably well together and will probably invent games of their own to play. The outdoor air seems fresher, the sunshine healthier, when a little boy or girl has a Poodle to go out and play with. A Poodle has that extra sense of humor that makes him appeal to all people, young and old, from every land.

Suggested Reading

The following books contain information of interest and value to anyone interested in Poodles and their care.

THE BOOK OF THE POODLE
By Anna Katherine Nicholas
ISBN 0-87666-736-1
TFH H-1033

Contents: Origin and Early History Of The Poodle. Early Poodles In The United States. History And Development Of The Toy Poodle. Important Kennels Of The Present Day. Poodles In Australia. Poodles In Canada. English Poodles Of The 1980's. Poodles In Europe. Poodles In Japan. Latin American Poodles. America's Top winning Best In Show Dog. Official Standard For The Poodle. Mrs. Hoyt Discusses The Poodle. Your Poodle As A Show Dog. Care, Clipping, And Trimming Of The Poodle Coat. The Poodle Puppy. Feeding Your Poodle. The Poodle As A Family Companion. Poodles In Obedience. Breeding Poodles. Responsibilities Of Poodle Breeders And Owners. Veterinarian's Corner.

Audience: For those in the Dog Fancy who want to own a book filled with details about the breed not to be found in any other publication. The author, a respected long-time breeder and eminent dog show judge, details the history of the Poodle. In addition, the text discusses over 40 present-day kennels, giving the exhibiting and breeding history of each kennel. A marvelous visual chronicle of Poodle exhibiting, displaying representative old and new champions. Special sections on breeding and a veterinarian's corner add to this unique volume's value. High school and above.
Hard cover, 8½ x 11", 528 pages
143 full-color photos, 860 black and white photos

YOU AND YOUR POODLE
By Mollie Skelton
ISBN 0-87666-362-5
TFH PS-641

Contents: Choosing A Poodle. Training Your Poodle Puppy. Feeding And General Care. Grooming Your Poodle. The Dutch Clip. The Working Clip. The Puppy Clip. The English Saddle Clip And The Continental Clip. Choosing A Show Quality Puppy. Training The Puppy For Show.

Audience: For the Poodle pet owner and prospective buyer this book gives invaluable advice to anyone who has had a question concerning the care and management of a Poodle.
Hard cover; 8½ x 5"; 127 pages
93 black and white photos; 6 line illustrations

CLIP AND GROOM
YOUR OWN POODLE
By William La Fetra
ISBN 0-87666-356-0
TFH H-926

Contents: Your Poodle's Coat. Necessary Grooming Equipment. Brushing. Bathing And Drying. How To Clip Your Poodle. The Basic Clip. The Puppy Clip. The Show Clips. The Dutch Clip. The Lamb Clip. The Town And Country Clip. The Summer Clip. The Kennel Clip. Mustaches And Color Tinting. The Professional Dog Groomer. Mimic And Fun Clips.

Audience: For the expert and beginner alike. By following the step-by-step illustrated and simply written directions, the Poodle owner can learn to clip and groom all types and sizes of Poodle.
Hard cover; 8½ x 11"; 80 pages
76 black and white photos; 27 color photos